JUNGLE WARFARE

by

Wallace B. Black
and
Jean F. Blashfield

CRESTWOOD HOUSE
New York

Maxwell Macmillan Canada
Toronto

Maxwell Macmillan International
New York Oxford Singapore Sydney

Library of Congress Cataloging-in-Publication Data

Black, Wallace B.
    Jungle warfare / by Wallace B. Black and Jean F. Blashfield. —
1st ed.
      p.   cm. — (World War II 50th anniversary series)
Includes index.
    Summary: Describes jungle warfare in Southeast Asia and the islands of
the Pacific during World War II.
    ISBN 0-89686-563-0
    1. World War, 1939-1945 — Jungle warfare — Asia, Southeastern —
Juvenile literature. 2. World War, 1939-1945 — Jungle warfare — Pacific
Area — Juvenile literature. [1. World War, 1939-1945 — Jungle warfare —
Asia, Southeastern. 2. World War, 1939-1945 — Jungle warfare — Pacific
Area.] I. Blashfield, Jean F. II. Title. III. Series: Black, Wallace B. World
War II 50th anniversary series.
D767.B53 1992
940.54'25—dc20

                      JUVENILE
                      D
                      767
                      .B53
                      1992

91-31533
CIP
AC

Created and produced by B & B Publishing, Inc.

Picture Credits
Dave Conant, map - page 9
Imperial War Museum - pages 18, 21, 22, 26, 36, 43, 45 top, center left
National Archives - pages 4, 6, 8, 11, 13, 15, 16, 25, 28, 30, 38-39, 40, 41, 44
United States Air Force - pages 3, 12, 31, 32, 33, 45 center right, bottom

**CRESTWOOD
HOUSE**

Macmillan Publishing Company
866 Third Avenue
New York, NY 10022

Maxwell Macmillan Canada, Inc.
1200 Eglinton Avenue East
Suite 200
Don Mills, Ontario M3C 3N1

Macmillan Publishing Company is part of the Maxwell Communication Group of Companies.

Printed in the United States of America

First Edition

10 9 8 7 6 5 4 3 2 1

CONTENTS

A U.S. convoy climbs the famous 21-curve section of the Burma Road as the trucks head into China with supplies.

Chapter 1

JAPAN INVADES BURMA

World War II jungle warfare started soon after Japan's treacherous bombing of Pearl Harbor on December 7, 1941. Even as the bombs were dropping on Hawaii, Japan had begun the conquest of much of Southeast Asia and the islands of the South Pacific. Japanese armies began storming through the jungles of Siam (Thailand), the Malay Peninsula and the Philippine Islands a few days later.

By mid-1942, the Japanese invasion of jungle lands included Burma, the Malay Peninsula, the islands of the Dutch East Indies, the Solomon Islands, New Guinea and other Pacific islands. The Japanese had been preparing for all-out war for years. The British and Dutch and their colonial forces in India, Burma and the Dutch East Indies were poorly prepared to fight any kind of a war—much less a war in the jungle.

Japan Strikes on Many Fronts

The Japanese war in Southeast Asia came about because of two main conditions. First of all, Japan was a small country with a large population. It wanted space to expand, and its growing industrial and military activities needed more natural resources such as oil, rubber, iron ore and coal. A second factor was the dominant position of European countries and the United States in Asian affairs. Japan felt that Asians should handle Asian affairs.

So the purpose of Japan's waging war against the United States, Great Britain, the Netherlands and their

Pacific and Southeast Asian colonies was twofold. First of all was the desire to expand. Then Japan wanted to drive the Westerners out of Asia.

To accomplish these goals the Japanese attacked targets throughout the entire Pacific region and Southeast Asia. Each target was a stepping-stone to the next one. Burma was a target of great importance, one that required immediate conquest.

Burma — A Key to Victory

China, Japan's number-one enemy and object for conquest, was being supplied through Burma. Japan had been at war with China since 1937. Using the famous Burma Road, military supplies were brought to western China. Japan's immediate goal in Burma was close to the road. Without the military supplies delivered through Burma, the conquest of all of China by Japan could come about more quickly.

Control of Burma would also open the door for attack on India. India, Burma's neighbor to the northwest, had a

A photograph captured from enemy soldiers shows Japanese troops using a flamethrower against a British defensive positions in Burma.

population of more than 600 million people. It was vast in both size and natural resources. India was considered the jewel of the British Empire.

An English colony for more than 150 years, India provided Great Britain with the resources to support British military and trade activities throughout all of Asia. As long as India was controlled by Great Britain, Japan could not achieve its goals.

Japan Starts Burma Offensive

The Japanese attacked bases in southern Burma in mid-January 1942. They advanced rapidly northward until June of that year. They drove the British, Chinese and Burmese forces northward with their lightning advance until they were stopped by the monsoon season. Each year in Burma and India, from May until October, heavy rains and winds can cause as much as 200 inches of rain to fall. Roads become impassable and fighting is almost impossible.

On March 10, an American, Lieutenant General Joseph W. "Vinegar Joe" Stilwell, was made chief of staff of the Chinese armies in southwest China and Burma. Ten days later he was made commander of all U.S. forces in Southeast Asia. He led two Chinese armies into Burma to help the British fight the Japanese. General J. W. Slim commanded the British, Indian and Burmese armies in western Burma. None of these forces was able to stop the advancing Japanese.

Japanese Invasion a Success

By the month of May, the Japanese were in complete control of most of Burma. The British, Indian and Chinese armies had been defeated and had retreated northward. The Allied armies could offer little resistance to the advancing Japanese.

Finally, on May 6, General Stilwell and his staff reached Mandalay in central Burma. Believing that a commander

General Stilwell (second from left) and his party reach the end of the road before starting their long march from Burma in May of 1942.

should stay with his troops, Stilwell refused to be evacuated by air. He led his staff and a small group of soldiers and civilians northward on foot. Through heavy monsoon rains, they marched for 20 days until reaching safety in the Assam region of India.

In General Stilwell's own words, "We took one hell of a beating." The Japanese now controlled the Burma Road to China and were moving troops northward in Burma in preparation for an attack on India.

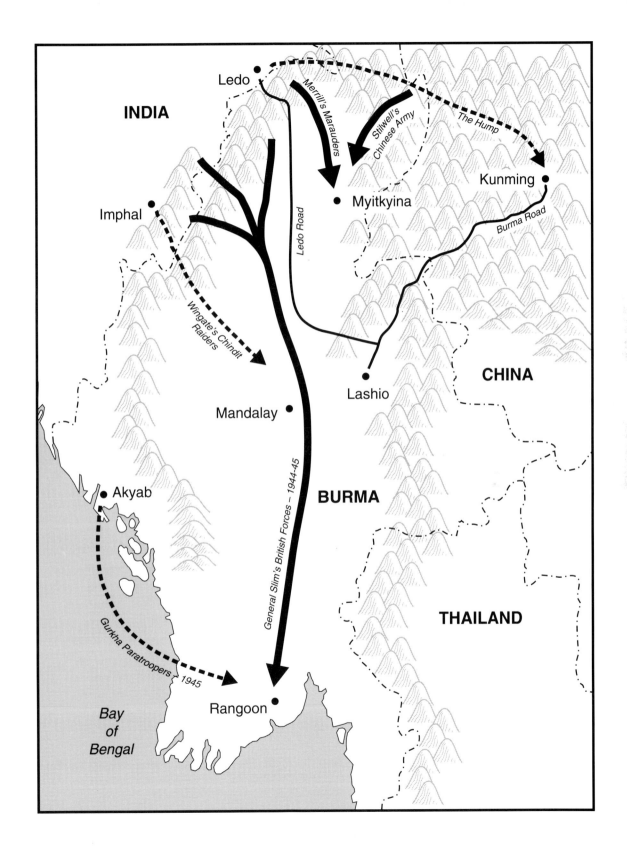

Chapter 2

VINEGAR JOE STILWELL

Lieutenant General Joseph W. Stilwell earned his nickname, Vinegar Joe, by being tough, hard-nosed and very blunt. A brilliant soldier, he was an equally poor diplomat but was always highly respected.

As World War II started, General Stilwell was one of the U.S. Army's highest ranking generals. He was called to Washington to meet with the secretary of war, Henry Stimson. Stilwell was asked if he would go to China and help command and train the Chinese army. His answer was, "I'll go where I'm sent." In February 1942 he left for the Far East to meet with Generalissimo Chiang Kai-shek, the head of the Chinese government.

A Career Soldier

Stilwell began his military career at the United States Military Academy at West Point, New York. He graduated in 1904 and became a second lieutenant in the infantry. A good officer and a good soldier, Stilwell advanced steadily but slowly.

As the years passed he served in China as a language specialist and intelligence officer several times. By far the most knowledgeable military expert on China, Stilwell was chosen to work with the Chinese armies in 1942. Throughout most of the war years he served as the commanding general of all U.S. forces in China, Burma and India, the countries known as the CBI. He also served as chief of staff of the Chinese armies in Burma.

Constant Battles with "Peanut"

There was continual disagreement between Stilwell and China's leader, Chiang Kai-shek, whom Stilwell called "Peanut." The two leaders had little respect for each other.

About 10,000 Chinese soldiers had been trapped in India after the fall of Burma. Stilwell wanted to retrain them in India to fight in Burma once again. Chiang wanted him to train troops to fight the Japanese in China.

Frequently Chiang would issue orders contrary to Stilwell's. Chiang kept demanding more and more supplies be flown to China for fighting the Japanese in eastern China. Stilwell needed supplies to fight in Burma. He believed that many of the supplies sent to China were not being put to use, but were being stored to be used to fight the Chinese Communists when the war was over.

Finally, after years of fighting each other, in late 1944 Chiang Kai-shek demanded that Stilwell be removed. President Franklin D. Roosevelt and U.S. Army Chief of Staff George Marshall had no alternative but to agree.

Generalissimo and Madame Chiang Kai-shek and General Stilwell share a rare happy moment.

Top Allied generals confer on strategy for the Burma campaign:
(left to right) Lieutenant General Henry "Hap" Arnold, General Claire
Chennault, General Joseph Stilwell, British Field Marshal Sir John Dill
and Brigadier General Clayton L. Bissell

Battling Generals

In addition to problems with Chiang Kai-shek, Vinegar
Joe had a running battle with General Claire Chennault of
Flying Tigers fame. The Flying Tigers had been fighting the
Japanese air force for six months in Burma and China since
December 1941. On July 4, 1942, they became part of the
U.S. Army Air Force (USAAF). At that time Chennault was
made a brigadier general in command of the China Air Task
Force. He reported to General Stilwell.

Stilwell and the British generals thought the answer to
victory over the Japanese in southeast Asia was to drive
them out of Burma. Chennault and Chiang Kai-shek thought
it was more important to drive the Japanese eastward out
of China.

This disagreement on war plans led to constant battles between the two officers and with Chiang. Chennault was a popular figure back in the United States because of his success with the Flying Tigers. He had strong backing in the press and from President Roosevelt. Stilwell had the backing of the British as well as support from U.S. Army Chief of Staff Marshall in Washington.

Chennault believed he could build a force that would drive the Japanese from China. He demanded the lion's share of supplies that were flown in from India to supply his air force and to build airfields.

Chennault bypassed Stilwell and appealed directly to President Roosevelt. He received the go-ahead for his plans. He started building up the new Fourteenth Air Force and bases in central China in preparation for his planned aerial defeat of the Japanese.

In the long run Chennault's activities resulted in a strong counteroffensive by the Japanese, which wiped out the forward bases he had built. Since Chennault's plan had failed, Stilwell and the British were able to continue the long-delayed drive against the Japanese in Burma.

Chinese soldier guards the tiger-nosed P-40s of the China Air Task Force.

Chapter 3

Jungle Misery

Fighting in the jungles of Burma was miserable for both sides. The climate in Burma is one of the worst in the world. There is always heavy rain during the monsoon season. The temperature can soar as high as 130° F.

In addition to the climate, the mountains and jungles of Burma presented almost insurmountable obstacles. Soldiers in Burma had to scale rugged mountain ranges while at the same time hacking their way through jungle so heavy that it blocked out the sun. At the bottom of mountain valleys were roaring streams that became completely impassable rivers during the monsoon. Heavy bamboo, elephant grass and jungle growth of every kind had to be cut away to make paths through the jungle.

Insects, Snakes, Leeches and Disease

As a jungle fighter battled the terrain and torrential rains, he had other problems. Insects would bite and sting, and blood-sucking leeches several inches long would attach themselves to a soldier's body as he struggled through waist-deep mud or towering vegetation. Jungle diseases caused more casualties than guns and bombs. Dysentery, malaria, dengue fever and exhaustion could wipe out entire battalions. Poisonous snakes such as the krait or cobra were abundant.

Japanese Skilled at Jungle Warfare

Along with the enemies provided by nature, there were always the Japanese jungle fighters. In the early days of the Burmese conflict the Japanese held almost the entire

American medics treat casualties at a base deep in the Burmese jungle.

country. They controlled the roads and the railways and had large numbers of experienced troops. The Japanese regular army soldiers were well disciplined and would rather die than surrender. They forced the defending British and Chinese armies to retreat northward following the initial invasion.

As the war in Burma continued to expand, the Japanese forces prepared to invade India. Soon they were concentrated in bases near cities and used the main roads and railways for transportation. The jungles were left to the Allied guerrilla fighters.

Allies Learn to Use the Jungle

In 1943 and 1944, Allied armies learned the ways of jungle fighting. The tide began to turn. Helped by native tribes, Allied soldiers learned how to find their way through the trackless jungle. The jungle hid them from the enemy as they drove deep behind enemy lines. Battling opponents often could not see the enemy even when they were only a few feet away.

Two U.S. combat photographers cross a jungle stream as they follow Merrill's Marauders.

Heavy bamboo was used to build fortifications to protect defenders from enemy fire. Long, sharpened bamboo spears called *punji sticks* were placed on jungle trails to stab unsuspecting Japanese soldiers. Openings to fire through were chopped out of the heavy jungle growth to ambush Japanese troops and vehicles as they advanced down trails and roads.

But jungle fighters could last in combat only a short time. Even well-trained, native troops could not last more than 90 days in combat. Exhaustion or disease would take over. Those who experienced all of the horrors of war felt that jungle warfare was the worst possible ordeal they could imagine.

Chapter 4

WINGATE'S CHINDIT RAIDERS

According to many who served with him, British general Orde Wingate was half genius and half madman. Wingate found his place in history as he led guerrilla forces against the Japanese in Burma during World War II. Before the war he had served as a captain in Palestine as the British fought the Arabs to bring peace in that country. For his outstanding services there he was awarded the DSO (Distinguished Service Order) medal.

Sent back to a desk job in London, Wingate thought he had reached a deadend. The start of World War II ended that worry. General Archibald Wavell, commander in chief of the British in the Middle East, ordered Wingate to Ethiopia to help drive the Italians from that African country. With Great Britain now at war with Italy as well as Germany, the Italians in Ethiopia had attacked British territories in East Africa.

Wingate rapidly organized a guerrilla army called the Gideon Force. They carried out acts of sabotage and attacked the Italians. Wingate and his small army chased the Italians as they retreated. He succeeded in capturing over 15,000 of them.

Even when he was successful, Wingate would get into trouble. He tried to enter into the politics of now-free Ethiopia and argued with everyone. He was relieved of his command and sent to Egypt.

Completely depressed and ill with malaria and physical exhaustion, Wingate attempted suicide by cutting his throat. Prompt medical care saved his life. Demoted to major, he was sent back to Great Britain.

Wingate Comes to Burma

Once again his old friend General Wavell came to Wingate's rescue. Now in command of the British army in India, Wavell sent for Wingate. He was to lead guerrilla forces against the Japanese in Burma.

His first effort, called Operation Longcloth, was made up of British, Gurkhas (soldiers from Nepal) and Burmese troops. Three thousand strong, they were formed into eight columns and each penetrated deep into Japanese-held territory in Burma. They were called Chindits, after the winged stone dragons that guard Burmese temples.

In February of 1943 the Chindits attacked. They disrupted enemy supply lines, blowing up railroad tracks and bridges and ambushing supply trucks. The Chindits proved that British and Indian troops could sneak behind the Japanese lines to fight the enemy.

Some of Wingate's Chindit raiders carry a wounded companion on a jungle trail in Burma.

Unfortunately, bad luck followed Wingate and his Chindits. Nearly trapped by superior Japanese forces, they suffered many casualties. The Chindits broke up into small groups and found their way back to safety in India. Of the original 3,000 Chindits, 883 were lost to enemy action or disease. Fewer than 1,000 men were able to fight again.

Failure Leads to Success

Wingate was not modest. His written reports emphasized his belief that Chindit guerrilla-type forces could successfully defeat the Japanese. Friendly war correspondents who admired his daring tactics wrote glowing stories about Wingate, his Chindits and his theories.

These news stories and Wingate's reports came to the attention of the British prime minister, Winston Churchill. He ordered Wingate to come to London to discuss future plans for Burma.

Wingate convinced Churchill that his plans for guerrilla action in Burma would succeed. He was given the rank of major general and sent back to India with complete authority and the resources to carry out his plans. A new Chindit group called Wingate's Special Force was formed.

The Mission Called Thursday

Just four months after the first Chindit mission, Wingate was ready to go back into Burma. Under the overall command of Lieutenant General Stilwell, three forces were to go into action. A Chinese army trained in India was to attack and beat back the Japanese in northern Burma. A second force, made up of U.S. Army Engineers, was to follow close behind, building the Ledo Road that would link up with the old Burma Road.

The third force was Wingate's. It was made up of more than 23,000 men in six brigades. A seventh brigade, the U.S. Army 5307th Composite Unit (Provisional), was also a part of Wingate's force.

The Japanese 18th Division, under the command of the brilliant Japanese general Shinichi Tanaka, was fighting for control of north Burma. While Stilwell's Chinese army attacked the Japanese from the north, Wingate's Operation Thursday was to fly in behind the Japanese lines. The Chindits and the 5307th were to disrupt enemy communcations, attack enemy bases and destroy supplies, fuel and munitions.

Wingate's Forces Prepare for Action

During their first mission, the Chindits had walked through the mountainous jungles of Burma to find the enemy. Once there, deep in the jungle and with no air support, they fought the Japanese. Short of supplies, they were outnumbered and outfought by a large, well-trained Japanese force. They had to walk out through the jungle, beset by rain, mud, insects and disease. These disastrous tactics had to be changed.

The first new rule Wingate laid down was that deep-penetration forces needed complete air support. The troops, along with their equipment and supplies, had to be flown in. Once in place, they had to build airstrips and air-drop areas so that they could be supplied by air. For his next operation, Wingate wanted his own air transport, fighters and bombers.

Troops operating in the jungle deep behind enemy lines could function efficiently for only about 90 days. Wingate's second new rule was that after that time the jungle fighters were to be flown out for rest and recuperation.

Operation Thursday Takes Off

On March 5, 1944, Wingate's second Burmese mission got under way. U.S. P-51 fighters and B-25 medium bombers hit selected targets to prepare the way. Later that night, USAAF C-47s towing troop-carrying gliders took off. Although some gliders were lost on the way and others crashed on landing, hundreds of Chindits and their equipment landed safely. Well behind enemy lines, their new base was called Broadway.

More Chindits followed, landing at other hidden bases. Wingate's task was to set up a strong force at each of these points. Headquarters, communications and supply units were established at each base and small, well-hidden airstrips were constructed. Roving bands of Chindits would attack enemy bases in the rear area. Their ambushes and surprise attacks helped to prevent reinforcements and needed supplies from reaching the Japanese 18th Division advance units.

U.S. supplies parachute to waiting Chindit troops at their base behind Japanese lines.

General Wingate (center) *and his staff brief Air Commando pilots for a mission over Burma. USAAF Air Commando Group commander Colonel Phil Cochran stands at Wingate's left.*

Wingate Killed in Crash

As March drew to a close, about 10,000 Chindits were in position at bases behind Japanese lines. Wingate flew in to these forward bases to help plan the guerrilla campaign. Already in action, the raiders were fighting fierce battles with Japanese patrols. Chindit assault teams bombed bridges and barricaded roads and railroad tracks. Operation Thursday was off to a good start.

On March 24, 1944, Wingate flew in to meet with Brigadier B. E. Ferguson, commander of the 16th Brigade. They were planning attacks on Japanese airfields. That night Wingate boarded an American B-25 to return to his headquarters in India. His plane never arrived.

Wingate was declared missing on March 26, and his wrecked plane was discovered the next day. Major General W. D. A. Lentaigne, Wingate's deputy, assumed command of the Special Force. The Chindits fought on.

Chapter 5

MERRILL'S MARAUDERS

The U.S. Army group that was to become a part of Wingate's Special Force in their missions in the jungles of Burma was known as Merrill's Marauders. It was officially called the 5307th Composite Unit (Provisional), U.S. Army. This meant that the group was made up of men with a variety of skills who had been drawn from many different units. The "provisional" meant that it was temporary.

The original 3,000 Marauders were volunteers from units in the South Pacific who were experienced in jungle fighting. Training under miserable conditions in a British camp in the middle of India, the men's morale was a constant problem.

Whenever the Marauders visited local villages the military police had their hands full with the hard-drinking and generally disorderly soldiers of the 5307th seeking relief from boredom. While they were being trained, the group had no identifiable character. Its name was meaningless and they had no permanent leader. It had no unit insignia and had no understanding of what its goal or purpose was. But this nondescript outfit grew together and became a skilled jungle-fighting infantry brigade.

Frank Merrill Takes Command

Although part of Wingate's Special Force for a short time, the 5307th was still under the command of General Stilwell. Brigadier General Frank Merrill was a friend of Stilwell's and had been a part of the group that had walked out of Burma with him. General Stilwell appointed Merrill to command the 5307th.

Withdrawn from Wingate's Special Force, the 5307th was sent to Assam to prepare for the attack on northern Burma. The unit was to support the Chinese forces trained by Stilwell. The attack on the Japanese 18th Division began in February 1944.

The Battle of Walawbum Village

The main goal of the spring 1944 campaign in north Burma was to capture the city of Myitkyina (pronounced MIT-chin-ar) and its airports. This city was a transportation center that supplied the Japanese in northern Burma. The new Ledo Road would need to be routed through this city. Capturing its airfields would force Japanese air force units to operate from bases much farther south.

To accomplish this, General Stilwell sent his Chinese-American 30th Division, supported by Merrill's force, into action. They advanced swiftly and attacked General Tanaka's 18th Division on a broad front. To the south, behind the enemy lines, Wingate's Chindits were attacking the enemy's supply lines. The Japanese withdrew some troops from the main battle to fight the Chindits.

But as the 30th Division entered the Hukawng Valley on the road to Myitkyina, it met fierce Japanese resistance. As part of Stilwell's plan, Merrill's force, marching through thick jungle, took up a position at the rear of the Japanese. They attacked and set up a strong defensive position at the village of Walawbum to block a Japanese retreat.

General Tanaka, reversing directions, attacked Walawbum in force. Bayonet charges accompanied by the Japanese war cry of *Banzai!* were repeated again and again as the Japanese attacked Merrill's positions. The fight had lasted for three days when Tanaka realized he could not win the battle. So he ordered a retreat and slipped away to the south.

A U.S. General Sherman tank in northern Burma. American and Chinese troops watch as the tank's 75-mm cannon blasts Japanese positions.

Merrill's Marauders are Named

Stilwell's Chinese army and the supporting 5307th Composite Unit were now in control of the Hukawng Valley. As they rested and licked their wounds, an eager war correspondent was at the front writing up the story of the battle. Disgusted with the official name — the 5307th Composite — he suggested a name that would catch the eye of the public and the military as well. He called them Merrill's Marauders. That name followed this heroic group into history.

Planning a rapid follow-up to the success at Walawbum, Stilwell ordered the Marauders to divide their force. One battalion was to follow Tanaka's retreating Japanese troops. A second battalion was to execute a hook movement to again attack the Japanese from the rear, cutting their supply lines.

The second battalion performed perfectly. As they completed the hook around the Japanese lines, they chanced upon a large supply depot and service units. The Japanese were not prepared for battle. This base was demolished, and hundreds of Japanese were killed or wounded.

Up to this time the Marauders had fought 13 actions as they advanced southward. They had killed over 800 of the enemy while losing only a handful of their own men. But they were suffering other casualties from disease. There was also the problem of psychological breakdown in men not ready for the blood and death of battle.

General Merrill Has a Heart Attack

The days that followed the early successes of the Marauders were filled with constant combat. General Tanaka's 18th Division, seasoned and experienced, recovered from each defeat to fight back more fiercely than ever. Although

A Marauder patrol crossing a river in northern Burma

short of supplies and attacked from front and rear and from the air, the Japanese gave up ground slowly.

The Marauders' first battalion was a casualty of Tanaka's veteran troops. Reserve Japanese regiments inflicted heavy casualties as they attacked the advance units of the Marauders. As the Marauders retreated before the advancing Japanese, the retreat became a rout that did not stop until it reached battalion headquarters. There General Merrill and his staff brought the retreat to a halt.

Then the Marauders turned and began 36 hours of bayonet charges and hand-to-hand fighting in jungle so thick that the opposing lines were often just a few feet apart. But the Marauders held on. Supplies and reinforcements were flown in. However, a battle-weary and exhausted General Merrill collapsed. Fighting hard to the last minute, he suffered a heart attack and was flown out of the combat zone. Colonel Charles N. Hunter assumed command.

The Marauders Begin to Weaken

The Marauders had fought through some of the worst jungles in the world. Rugged mountains and roaring streams and rivers had been crossed as they pursued and battled Tanaka's crack 18th Division. They were exhausted, morale was low, they had lost their leader and over half of the men were casualties.

As the final battles for Myitkyina approached, the unit was down to less than half its strength. Wounded and sick men were brought back to the front lines before they were well. But they still fought on.

By the middle of May, General Merrill had recovered sufficiently to return to take command of the Marauders. On May 15, a combined operation by Chinese, Kachin Burmese tribesmen and American Marauders was ready for an attack on the Myitkyina airfields. On May 16, Colonel Hunter led the attacking force. After a hard fight the airfields were captured.

The dense jungles of Burma provided excellent concealment from the enemy.

The next day Merrill was hit with another heart attack. He was never able to return to combat. As the monsoon weather began to bear down on Burma, the fortunes of the Marauders went further downhill. Dysentery and other jungle diseases took their toll.

Taken out of battle for a well-earned rest, Merrill's Marauders had lived up to Colonel Hunter's description of them in every way. He called them "the most beat upon, most misunderstood, most mishandled, most written-about, most heroic, yet most unrewarded regimental-sized unit in World War II."

Chapter 6

THE U.S. AIR FORCE IN THE CBI

An American air force came to the CBI unofficially during the summer of 1941 in the form of the Flying Tigers. Following the declaration of war with Japan in December 1941, regular U.S. Army Air Force units began to arrive in India and China in steadily growing numbers. American airmen played a key role in helping defeat the Japanese in China, Burma and India.

The air force carried the jungle fighters far behind enemy lines. It flew out the sick and wounded. The C-46, C-47 and C-54 transports carried troops and the tools of war over mountain ranges. The P-40 and P-51 fighters gave support to Wingate's Chindit raiders and Merrill's Marauders in the jungles below. And B-24, B-25 and B-29 bombers dumped tons of bombs on enemy targets near and far.

Chinese Air Force Destroyed

China was steadily losing its war with Japan. The Chinese air force had been shot to pieces. They needed help in rebuilding an air force and they needed it before Japan took over all of China.

Retired U.S. Army Air Corps general Chennault had been hired by the Chinese in 1937 to help train their air force. In spite of his great experience and skill, Chennault could do little with the limited resources available. Working with the Chinese leaders, Generalissimo Chiang Kai-shek and Chiang's brother-in-law, T. V. Soong, Chennault helped organize the American Volunteer Group (AVG).

The AVG, which came to be known as the Flying Tigers, was made up of U.S. Army, Navy and Marine pilots and ground crews. Released from duty in the U.S. armed forces, they were hired by the Chinese government to fight the Japanese.

Chennault, now a colonel in the Chinese air force, commanded this colorful group of thrill-seeking young pilots. By December 1941 he had a force of 100 American P-40 Warhawk fighter planes and was busy training the pilots to fly them in combat.

The Flying Tigers and the Burma Road

With the Japanese in control of all major Chinese seaports, supplies for the Chinese armies had to come through Burma. After the supplies had been landed at Rangoon, everything had to be carried north by rail to Lashio in eastern Burma and then 700 miles by truck over the Burma Road. This famous road ran through mountains and jungles to Kunming, China. It was the job of the Flying Tigers to keep the route open.

General Chennault (rear) *and General Stilwell* (center) *with several airmen alongside a Flying Tiger P-40 at a base in China*

Air Commando gliders prepare for a mission over Burma.

Soon after the start of all-out war between Japan and the Allies, Japan struck in Burma. Flying from jungle bases in Burma and from Kunming, China, the Flying Tigers went into action. They attacked formations of Japanese bombers as they tried to bomb Burmese cities. With .50-caliber guns spitting fire, the shark-nosed P-40s scored victory after victory. While fighting to keep the jungle highway to China open, the Flying Tigers shot down over 350 Japanese planes and lost only 12 P-40s to enemy action.

For six months the Flying Tigers fought, and some died, as they flew over the Burmese jungles. Finally, on July 4, 1942, the AVG was disbanded. Its leader, Claire Chennault, was made a brigadier general in the U.S. Army Air Force. Many of the Flying Tigers' pilots and ground crews became part of the newly formed China Air Task Force commanded by Chennault.

The First Air Commando Group

In the spring of 1944 General Wingate and his Chindit raiders needed and demanded air support. They needed a small air force they could depend on and control. Two young Americans, Colonel Phil Cochran and Colonel Johnny Alison, were given the job of commanding the air force's No. 1 Air Commando Group to provide that air support.

This elite group consisted of 30 P-51 fighters, 12 B-25 medium bombers, 25 C-47 transports, over 100 light aircraft and more than 200 gliders. Supported by a large maintenance squadron, this unusual group gave its all for General Wingate and the Chindits. Colonel Cochran, a tough fighter pilot, directed this heroic group with great skill and success.

The Air Commando Group delivered fighter and bomber attacks whenever and wherever they were needed. Their P-51s and B-25s bombed and strafed bridges and supply routes. Their C-47 transports and little two-seater L-5s flew men and supplies into the smallest and roughest fields imaginable. With every return trip they served as flying ambulances for the wounded and the sick.

Although other U.S. Army Air Force and Royal Air Force units gave service to the Allied troops in Burma, not one is remembered as fondly as the U.S. Air Commando Group.

Flying the Hump

Another important USAAF unit was the heroic India-China Wing of the U.S. Air Transport Command (ATC).

Airports in China and India were often built by civilian laborers. Chinese laborers are seen here breaking up rocks by hand as a C-47 transport flies overhead.

A pilot's view of the Hump. Air transport aircraft carrying supplies to China flew as high as 20,000 feet to avoid the rugged Himalayan mountain peaks.

It flew thousands of tons of supplies, ammunition and fuel from India to China. From 1942 to 1945 the wing delivered over 600,000 tons of supplies over the most dangerous route in the world — the Hump.

Flying the Hump involved taking off from bases near Chabua in northeast India and flying east for 500 miles to Kunming, China. The route took the courageous fliers over Himalayan mountain ranges in northern Burma towering more than 15,000 feet. The valleys in between the mountain ranges were filled with thick jungles, fierce head-hunting native tribes and deep, roaring rivers.

Weather over the Hump was completely unpredictable. Heavy turbulence, 200-mile-per-hour winds, ice, and torrential rains made every trip a challenge. And there were always Japanese fighters to contend with. The most dangerous sections of the Hump were said to be paved with aluminum — the aluminum wings and fuselages of the hundreds of aircraft that had crashed.

Flying the Hump in C-46s, C-47s and C-54s was a costly proposition. Crude airfields had to be scratched out of the Indian jungles. Shortage of equipment and supplies made keeping the aircraft flyable a serious problem. When the ATC's job was finished in 1945, the Hump had cost the lives of over 1,000 crew members, and some 600 planes had crashed.

B-29s and the 20th Air Force

In September 1944 General Curtis LeMay brought the 20th Bomber Command and its B-29s (called Super-Fortresses) to the CBI. He was a tough, cigar-chewing B-17 commander from the U.S. Eighth Air Force in England. The 20th's mission was to bomb Japanese-held cities and bases in Southeast Asia and on the mainland of Japan. Flying 20,000 feet above the jungle fighters below, the B-29s did their part by bombing the enemy's supply lines.

Chapter 7

THE OSS IN BURMA

The Office of Strategic Services (OSS) was a forerunner of the Central Intelligence Agency (CIA) we know today. Although it was most active in Europe during World War II, it also played a vital role in Burma. The OSS was formed in 1942 by General William J. "Wild Bill" Donovan. The organization's main job was to send well-trained and equipped U.S. and hired foreign agents behind enemy lines. Agents radioed back important information, committed acts of espionage and sabotage, and disrupted and fought the enemy in any way they could.

An OSS team of agents, once delivered into Burma, was expected to carry out these dangerous tasks. They were also to recruit, train, arm and direct Burmese natives in fighting the Japanese. An agent's job was difficult and dangerous. If caught, he could be executed as a spy.

Commanded by Colonel Carl Eifler, a tough regular-army career officer, OSS Detachment 101 was formed in the United States in the spring of 1942. When their training was complete, the 21 agents packed their supplies and set sail for India on May 28, 1942.

General Stilwell and his Chinese army associates did not trust the new OSS detachment. They did not understand its mission and its purpose and expected it to fail. But finally, Detachment 101 was given a secret base in northeast India. There the agents trained for six months for their daring missions to fight the Japanese behind the lines in Burma.

An OSS team picks up supplies dropped by parachute at a secret base deep in Burma.

Burmese Agents Hired

The most important thing for an agent operating behind enemy lines is to do so without being recognized as a spy. Naturally, being white Americans, no one in Detachment 101 met that requirement. They could plan, supply, train, lead and even operate in hiding in enemy territory. But they needed native agents to do the actual work among the enemy.

Agents who were Burmese or of mixed Burmese-English parentage were hired. Some had served in the Burmese army and others had worked in Burma. All spoke English and at least one Burmese dialect. Working with the OSS team, they were put through a crash training program in radio communications, use of explosives, map reading, and armed and unarmed combat.

The new trainees, however, knew more about how to proceed with the mission in Burma than their instructors did. They told the American agents about native customs and dress, habits of various tribes, life in the jungle, plants for food or medicine and more. Finally, on December 28, 1942, 101's first group was ready. Group A, commanded by Captain Jack Barnard, a Burmese-Anglo, flew into Fort Hertz, a British airstrip and base in northern Burma.

The Friendly Kachin Tribe

While at Fort Hertz, the agents made two important discoveries. First of all, they made contact with the local Kachin tribes and found that they were good friends of the British and Americans and hated the Japanese. From that time until the end of the war, the Kachin tribes were to be staunch allies.

They also discovered that walking any great distance in the jungle was impossible. They would have to fly or parachute their teams behind enemy lines whenever they could.

Soon the Group A agents were training the Kachins. They provided them with modern weapons and taught them how to use them. Some young Kachins were taught how to operate radios and other equipment. But most of all, they would serve as guides and teach the OSS teams the ways of the jungle.

Ambushes and Jungle Battles

The agents of Detachment 101 parachuted and flew into Chindit bases. Once on the scene, they disappeared into the jungles to spy on the Japanese and report their movements by radio. Whenever the opportunity presented itself, they would ambush a Japanese patrol, blow up a bridge or otherwise harass the enemy.

As the war progressed, OSS-trained Kachin forces of as many as 5,000 or more tribesmen were armed and trained and sent into the jungles to fight the Japanese. These guerrillas would make hit-and-run attacks on unsuspecting Japanese bases and troops. Detachment 101 continued to function in Burma until the end of the war.

Alert for Japanese snipers, two OSS agents lead a group of Kachin tribesmen behind Japanese lines.

Chapter 8

THE LAST CAMPAIGNS

The final conquest of Burma actually came in two parts and accomplished two separate goals. The first goal was to drive the Japanese out of northern Burma so that a land supply line could be opened from India to China. The second was to drive the Japanese out of southern Burma and reclaim its capital at Rangoon.

The Ledo-Burma Road

Since 1942 U.S. Army Engineers had been hacking away at the Burmese jungles to build the Ledo Road. Starting at Ledo in Assam, this new road was to be built through some of the most mountainous jungle terrain in the world. It was to join the Burma Road 500 miles to the south. At the same

A U.S. Army truck hauling an artillery piece crosses the border between China and Burma.

General Pick's engineers had to construct hundreds of bridges in addition to the giant task of building the road itself.

time the Burma Road had to be recaptured and repaired.

Over 60,000 engineers and native workers labored on this tremendous feat of engineering. Climbing up mountains 10,000 feet high and down to the depths of mountain gorges, they struggled through the jungles. Often just a few miles behind the battle lines, they were always in danger from enemy attacks as well as from the ever-present horrors of the Burma jungle.

Unable to bring in heavy equipment, they had only the lightest bulldozers available. The job of "moving mountains" seemed impossible. Hundreds of lives were lost to enemy action, disease and accidents. Hundreds of bridges had to be built. In some places the road was cut through solid rock. A sea of mud had to be battled during the monsoon seasons.

General Lewis A. Pick of the U.S. Army Engineers was in charge of this almost unbelievable project. His troops called the road Pick's Pike. Driving ahead at the rate of one mile a day, the general would not be stopped by Japanese snipers, the monsoon rains or dark of night. Supplies were delivered by everything from mule trains to parachutes, and the work went on.

Finally, on January 12, 1945, the job was completed. Led by General Pick, a truck convoy started the 1,030-mile trip to Kunming, China. A month later, supplies for China were being delivered by ground transport for the first time in almost three years.

The Ledo-Burma Road was a symbol of victory, even though it was in service for only ten months. When the war ended, it had delivered more than 50,000 tons of supplies to U.S. and Chinese forces still fighting the Japanese in China. After its completion it was renamed the Stilwell Road.

The Road to Rangoon

The other major campaign was the drive to recapture Rangoon and force the Japanese out of Burma. The "road to Mandalay" of song and story ran from Rangoon northward to the city of Mandalay in central Burma. British and Indian troops bound for victory were traveling that road in the other direction.

Pagodas (religious shrines) filled the ancient city of Mandalay. They served as miniature forts for Japanese snipers as the British forces tried to capture the city.

Under the command of Field Marshal Sir William Slim, British and Indian troops launched attacks during March 1945 against Mandalay and its heavily defended Fort Dufferin. General Slim's forces were victorious and continued on their southward march toward Rangoon. Charging down main roads and cutting trails through the jungle, they drove the retreating Japanese before them.

Mountbatten at Rangoon

Lord Louis Mountbatten, the Supreme Allied Commander of Southeast Asia, finally ordered an all-out attack on Rangoon. On May 1, 1945, British forces landed by air and from the sea just below the city. U.S. Army Air Force and British troop carrier squadrons dropped Gurkha para-

Gurkha paratroopers prepare to board a C-47 for a mission over Burma.

troopers on the landing area as the British navy conducted amphibious landings from the sea.

C-47s loaded with 1,000 Gurkha paratroopers took off from Akyab, 300 miles north of Rangoon, at four o'clock in the morning of May 1. They were to reach the drop zone at six o'clock. Under broken clouds the drop went as scheduled and the paratroopers landed.

At the same time, a huge fleet of over 100 British warships and landing craft were circling just offshore in the Andaman Sea below Rangoon. They hit the beach with amphibious landing forces and joined up with the Gurkhas.

Meeting only minimum resistance from the Japanese, the British forces fought their way toward the city of Rangoon. On May 3, the invading forces marched into the

British troops liberate the beautiful city of Prome from Japanese troops in May 1945.

capital city to find that the Japanese had fled. General Slim's army joined them a few days later, and the battle for Burma began to draw to a close.

War in central and north Burma and in China continued for some months. Die-hard Japanese troops by the tens of thousands were still fighting deep in the Burmese jungles. But jungle battles and the fighting in China were brought to an end on August 6, 1945, when the atomic bomb was dropped on Hiroshima in Japan.

Merrill's Marauders, Wingate's Chindits, the Flying Tigers, Stilwell, Chennault and thousands of other heroic jungle fighters had lived and died. At last the terrible years of jungle warfare in China, Burma and India were over.

A Closer Look at ...
LEADERS AND AIRCRAFT

Major General Orde Wingate (right) – In command of the British Special Services Detachment, Wingate developed long-range raids behind Japanese lines in Burma. He called his troops Chindit raiders after the stone lions that guarded Burmese temples. Following a brilliant career, he was killed in an airplane crash in Burma.

Field Marshal Sir William Joseph Slim (left) – In command of the British Fourteenth Army in Burma, Slim led the British army south to final victory at Rangoon in July of 1945. He was the most competent and respected British general in the CBI.

* *

Douglas C-54 Transport (right) – Known as the Skymaster, the C-54 was the first four-engine transport to see service in World War II. In 1944 it began to take over the job of flying the Hump from the overworked C-47s and C-46s. It could carry as many as 50 fully equipped troops or 20,000 pounds of cargo.

North American B-25 Medium Bomber (left) – Called the Mitchell, the B-25 saw service in every part of the world. Carrying a crew of six, it was armed with forward-firing machine guns or cannon and upper and tail gun turrets. It could carry a 3,000-pound bombload. It was used effectively by the Air Commando Group in Burma.

GLOSSARY

Allies The nations that joined together during World War II to defeat Germany, Japan and Italy: China, France, Great Britain, the Soviet Union and the United States.

ambush A surprise attack made from a hidden position.

amphibious troops Land and sea forces organized to work together during an invasion on an enemy shore.

bayonet A long knife designed to fit on the end of a rifle used in fighting.

CBI Abbreviation for the China-Burma-India area of war.

commandos A fighting force specially trained to make sudden destructive raids against an enemy.

drop zone An area designated as the point at which paratroopers or parachuted supplies should land.

espionage The act of spying on others, especially during time of war.

flamethrower A device that squirts a stream of flaming fuel toward a target.

glider An engineless aircraft that is designed to fly using air currents after being towed aloft by an airplane.

guerrilla warfare Fighting by loosely knit bands of people who use surprise and secrecy to harass an enemy.

monsoon A wind system that produces dry and wet seasons in India and Southeast Asia.

parachute A cloth canopy released from an enclosed pack used to slow the descent of a falling object.

paratrooper Soldiers trained to jump from aircraft using parachutes.

sabotage To damage or obstruct enemy troops, equipment and operations by using surprise tactics.

INDEX